# HAYDON

## AN ARTIST'S LIFE

# ROBERT PETERS

# HAYDON

## AN ARTIST'S LIFE

1989

Greensboro: Unicorn Press, Inc.

The author and publisher would like to thank Anita Richardson for typesetting, in 14/14 Deepdene, and McNaughton & Gunn for printing, on an acid-free sheet. Contributing to this publication from within the press were Alan Brilliant, Laurel Boyd, Sarah Lindsay, David Nikias, and Teo Savory.

Library of Congress Cataloging-in-Publication Data

Peters, Robert, 1924-
    Haydon: an artist's life / Robert Peters.
      p.  cm.
    ISBN 0-87775-219-2
    ISBN 0-87775-220-6 (pbk.)
    1. Haydon, Benjamin Robert, 1786-1846—Poetry.
      2. Painters—Great Britain—Poetry.    I. Title.
    PS3566.E756H34 1989
    811'.54—dc19                      88-35546

For reproduction rights, we are grateful to the National Portrait Gallery, London, for the cover death mask of Haydon by an unknown artist (c. 1820) and the frontspiece drawings of John Keats (1816) in Haydon's own hand.

Assistance for the publication of this edition was received from the National Endowment for the Arts, a Federal Agency.

Unicorn Press, Inc.
P.O. Box 3307
Greensboro, NC 27402

# TABLE OF CONTENTS

PART TWO: *This Rough World*

# BENJAMIN ROBERT HAYDON
## (1776-1846)

## An Artist's Life

Haydon, the historical painter, teacher, and writer, studied under Henry Fuseli, and was a friend of Keats, Hazlitt, Wordsworth, Lamb, the Carlyles, and Elizabeth Barrett Browning. Because of quarrels with leading Academicians, his ambitious works were seldom exhibited at the Royal Academy. His devotion to the highest ideals for his art led him into stark poverty. On four occasions he was humiliated and imprisoned for debt. The following poems are based in part on his superb *Autobiography* (1847).

I am grateful to the University of California at Irvine for grants in support of two visits to England to study Haydon's paintings; to Sarah Tinsley of the Tate Gallery for arranging for my viewing of five of Haydon's works, all of them in storage; to the Plymouth Museum for allowing me to examine nearly a dozen of Haydon's pictures, some them kept on rollers, and for supplying photographs; to Mr. Ian F. Outtrim, of London, a Haydon enthusiast who searched old newspaper morgues and the Westminster City Archives for contemporary items on Haydon's life and death, and who sent me snapshots of still existing London sites associated with Haydon; and to my dear friend Janine Dakyns, of London and Norwich, who has expedited my search for Haydon.

These are the primary texts I have consulted: *The Diary of Benjamin Robert Haydon*, 5 vols., edited by Willard Bissell Pope, (Cambridge, 1960-1963); *Life of Benjamin Robert Haydon, Historical Painter, from His Autobiography and Journals*, 3 vols., edited and compiled by Tom Taylor (London, 1853); *Benjamin Robert Haydon: Correspondence and Table-Talk*, 2 vols., edited by Frederic Wordsworth Haydon (London, 1876); Eric George, *The Life and Death of Benjamin Robert Haydon*, Oxford University Press (London, 1948); and Althea Hayter, *A Sultry Month: Scenes of London Literary Life in 1846* (London, 1965).

I am also grateful to the editors who have published poems from this work in their journals: to William Packard, *The New York Quarterly*; Anselm Parlatore, *Bluefish*; David Chorlton, *The Signal*; Mark Jarman and Robert McDowell, "The Reaper"; the editors of *Pearl*; and Harry Smith, *Pulpsmith*.

# HAYDON

# PART ONE

## Curses the Furies Breathe

*January 1, 1808*
A window snaps. Soughs of wind.
Four magpies on a snowy hedge.
Mother reads the embers.
I *know* that sharp nose,
those sunken cheeks.
I'm whipped across the mouth
with a fist of turnips.

* * * *

"They're not for mirth, these birds,"
Mother avers, short of breath,
in her bed,
after the bleeding.
"Fetch the Cheshire cat.
I've had three heart attacks."

We prop her in a wing-backed chair.
A servant brushes her hair.
I hold up a glass for her to see
where the parts should be.
"Harbingers," she exclaims, "of death.
*Four* magpies, then, my son.
Two sets of two, double titillation.
Spirit mathematics."

She flaps her black stole.
Her fingers metamorphosed
claw the chair.
"Snap their necks," she shouts.
"Snap their necks!"

We bathe her feet in hot vinegar.
When she screams, we rouse the house
and send for a surgeon.

"Children, I've lost my sight.
Where are you tonight?"

The surgeon delays.
He's at his house
warming his boots with lighted paper!
Mother is dying!
Mother is dead!

We close her eyes, her lips
and straighten her head.
I hold a mirror to her mouth,
then lock myself in her room.
I won't eat. I can't sleep.

A brutal hard-faced nurse
claims Mother's beaded purse.
I curse her.

I attire the snail-shell husk
of her body.

The coffin rumbles
along the rutted road to Ide
where my grandfather resides.
(Mother now lies by his side.)

I search the vault for rats.
I drape my red cravat over her heart.
O, I wish it were a ruby!
I bribe the sexton.
I do what I can.
This is not Baluchistan.

Imagine this Plymouthean
somewhat uncouth Promethean
young painter
having rehearsed his banter
and cut his chin shaving
and parboiled himself bathing
and having practiced bowing and scraping
(always with style).

See him on a brocade ottoman
talking to Lady Beaumont
local "beauty," the "font of virtue"
—no other words will do.
Oh, her deportments
and her puce (dish)habiliments!
I'm the "new man of the night!"
A "delight" at the Beaumont party
(so I'm told). A "rarity."

Down the table, matters political.
At this end, ones aesthetical.
Napoleon will offend the Tsar.
"By painting Lord Mulgrave you'll go far."
I leave the Beaumonts inflated and sure
my fame and destiny secure.

* * * *

Dear Reader, my judgments are sound.
I promise never to lead you around
either the mulberry or the apple tree.
Stay by me—if I appear vain, hear me again—
I'm so anxious to succeed in London.

David Wilkie advises me
to use raw oil for painting,
not oil boiled.
I moil and toil
yet my surfaces craze.
Wilkie, amazed,
advises I mend my ways.

I mix tints on pasteboard
and carry them to the Titians
for hints and comparisons
to both Nature and the Antique.
I first depict Joseph
cradling the Child,
with an ass attendant
and hovering angels,
distant pyramids . . . the color
harmonious, the forms circumspect:
color, light, shadow, impasto,
a fair imbroglio.
I seek pearly tints.
I've a lively eye for color.

The picture takes six months.
It's purchased by Mr. Thomas Hope
and hangs at Deepdene.

I'm a man of earnest feeling,
so you'll seldom hear me squealing
or railing against my fate.
My friends share my passions.
"Let's drink tea at Haydon's,
in his huge cups, in style."

O, Wilkie, Du Fresne, Callender, and Millingen.
And Lizzy, she shares our aesthetic propensities
and leaves her sex behind.
She's male in mind.
I think she's Wilkie's mistress.
She sits to him for pictures.

\* \* \* \*

Beware the Swiss painter Fuseli.
He'll turn your brains to jelly.

His English is guttural.
Alpine demons sepulchral
roll from his brain miasmic:
nightmares (frightening stallions)
Oberon, Puck, and haunted galleons.

Don't dislocate an arm
or wrench a femur from its joint
and call it "Style."
That's the point!
It's vile.
Nor would you paint six fingers
on a hand
and vow
that's how nature should depend
her simplest forms somehow.

* * * *

Fuseli cursed and swore,
was a compact five foot four, no more.
He stood firmly at his easel,
painted with his left hand, whistled,
never held his palette with his thumb.
Was myopic, but too vain for glasses.
He smeared hideous Prussian blue
on a Corybante's shoulder
deadened with a daub of ochre.
"By Gode," he'd chortle, "dat purple's
vary like Correggio's, by Gode!
Zee must astonish, move, dee-sturb
or your airt is no-zing, no-zing."
No drape was too baroque to slash,
no physiog too famed to trash.
He loved "High Art," seldom flattered sitters
and termed all "likenesses" mere "sparrow twitters."
Fuseli and I were intimates from that hour.

Alas, the Bower of Poverty and Pain—
my leprous life, then unforeseen
my whipped boil-encrusted back,
my scabaceous head. . . .

* * * *

Fourteen hours and more
rendering the Discobolos in chalk,
a self-assigned chore.
Arms and legs gigantic,
preparatory sketches frantic,
by candlelight, in a small book,
keeping the actual figure (in my mind)
always before me.

I stride a foot above the street!

* * * *

At Plymouth I find my father restored.
(Word had arrived he was dying.)
I delay returning to London.
I procure a pauper's corpse from a surgeon,
and late at night, by dim candlelight,
with scalpel and calipers
study the male anatomy.

My aunt whispers into my room
where I sit naked drawing.
She blows out the light.

"Benjamin's mad!
He's with Albinus on the floor,
stretched out on his belly reading."

13

I hope for news of a patron,
or of a lucrative commission.
All I have to show, alas,
are a few drawings,
some dry bones and drier muscles
correctly but unimaginatively rendered.

* * * *

Wilkie, now famous,
buys puce coats, talks grandly,
dresses as a dandy. His table
piles with the calling cards
of people of fashion
of people of no fashion
and of people of every fashion.
I am envious, yet I love him.

I am drawing skeletons
when something strikes him,
my rapt gaze, the skeletal holes
and the bones.
He sketches a caricature,
laughing loudly.
I respond badly:
"Let students, no matter how famous,
be cautious," I declare.
"Don't quiz external peculiarities
until you're certain of their verities."
He must be right. I must be wrong.

I'm in love with a charmer
I met at an inn.
Oh, her dimpled face, her creamy skin!
I call her "Olivia."
I read some Tasso and pine so
carving her name on trees,
and sigh so, lying on my elbow.
Alas, the Ideal always outruns the Real.
The Ideal always outruns the real.

Oh, Giorgione's finish
is rich and gemmy,
so gorgeous, deep-toned, and glittery.
I love The Woman Taken in Adultery.

* * * *

My heroic Roman Dentatus
stares fiercely
at a naked, frightened man
holding up a hand.

I paint, puzzle, paint,
rub out, and begin again.

I imagine it all, with Nature
as maidservant attendant.
And yet, I can not see
the hero's resplendent back.
And my model's arms seem so askew,
impalpable for an heroic context.
I don't know what to do.
If I draw from Phidias,
I've drawn from marble!
How hideous!

"Let's visit the Marbles!" says Wilkie
to cheer me.
He has Lord Elgin's permission.

* * * *

We pass through a hall,
through an open yard, and behind
to a damp, dirty pent-house and find
the Marbles strewn helter skelter.
Nature and Idea combine!
Never was bone so alive!
I examine the wrists of a female,
the radius and the ulna.
At the elbow the outer condyle
visibly affects the style.
The Theseus—every form displayed in action or repose.
The paired back-slabs vary, unclothed.
One springs forth from the shoulder blade
pushes up the spine, as Theseus rests on his elbow.
His belly is flat because, as he sits,
his bowels fall into his pelvis.

The belly of the Ilyssus, however, protrudes,
since he lies on his side.

An armpit muscle of a metope
in the instant action of darting out,
a muscle absent from the other armpit
because not wanted. . . . I shall faint!

I rise at five,
draw the Theseus from memory.
Fuseli dashes with me to the marbles:
"De Greeks were godes! De Greeks were godes!"

No, No, I am *not* mad
lying for hours on the floor
copying figures by the score.
The thing! done at once and forever!

\* \* \* \*

Almost daily, for half the year
I draw, astounded
by what Socrates looked on and Plato saw.
I often sketch til midnight,
turned out by the sleepy porter
holding a bleary rush-light.

\* \* \* \*

I spring from bed possessed,
and move through a dream,
impregnable to disease,
insensible to contempt, my spirit
frets my "pigmy body to decay,
and o'er informs its tenement of clay."
I'm conscious of the truths I've won.
"God," I pray, "bless your son."

A poised foot
signifies a gay mood.
Note the gold sweep
of those bare feet!
You hear your breath between
the interstices
of your own heart beats:
Phidias! How
the toes press down,
the upper joints not so.
The result? Flesh
rises about the nail
whilst the top and upper joints
maintain the form.
This is pure reason,
a probability bestowing motion.
Elsewhere the human form,
as rendered by the Greeks, uniform,
reveals a delicious slip
of the pectoral along the ribs.
Note that play of shapes
along the prone Ilyssus.
Oh, exquisite system!

Tomorrow will not be the same as today.
The garret is sludge-free
scrubbed by myself of stains
where the cat defecates
(the servant being off
attending a sick child).

Woke up intending
to reform my person
not the vanity-ridden husk
of the flat-bellied man I am
whose neckcloths are so stained
(whence comes this grease?)
no matter how much I scrub
and rub in jasmine.
I'll not eat a single cake
this entire day.

To reach my easel now
and the stone (imitating Fuseli)
on which I keep my paints
is possible without touching
a single item of furniture
(or lumber) misplaced.

By sketching in the missing limbs
of Theseus and Ilyssus
I seed my brain's landscape
with perfection
not the approximation.

The greatest blessing
brought to this country ever
are the Elgin marbles.

Half past four, dawn,
a ghastly hour,
yet one conducive to preliminaries:
a quick sketch of a mare's skull,
a cat femur
all towards inducing
the "right" feeling towards the marbles.
True principles elude me!
Spaces on my wall!
(I shall avoid breakfast
except for stale bread
crunched and swallowed whilst sketching)

* * * *

My night cap comes off.
Nevertheless, my hair is damp.
I must stop reading Boswell's *Johnson*.

Feathers from Homer's birds
quite fly out and quiver.
Virgil's are never
so beautiful or true.

If you subtract the times
(I rise from the hard floor)
both actual and metaphorical
from those times
when I reproach myself
for vanity
you shall comprehend my true nature:
I am a great bungler—
to wit: I finish a sketch
of a Centaur's back—a vulgar
porter-like form
true of men who carry burdens
(Centaurs, as you know,
are not intellectual!)
It's a good sketch
though I feel I'm slow,
a signal always (a proximate)
of a bloated brain
(stuffed with a venison dinner)
unexpected obstacles thicken
a miserable light fraught
by a cloud passing over, sickening
the skylight. Should Dentatus
wear a heeled sandal
or a sandal without a heel?
Should the ligatures of a torso
appear in upright figures
exactly as they appear
in the back side of a torso:
as any figure ascends
all markings unfold themselves
and are scarcely perceptible.
The ancients knew this.
I have just turned thirty-four.

Defeated, weeping,
I rub out the chest of my dying figure.
Rising, I brush against a marble.
It falls from its pedestal
cutting my leg. Much blood.
The Lapith haunch,
except for a single chip,
is intact. It screamed
where it fell.
PS: the more I study
the more I sense my own meanness.
I'll go no more to young men.
I return home
much improved in my studies
of the human back, and of horses.

\* \* \* \*

I model my journals
after Samuel Johnson's "diligence."
I reflect the tone always
of my favorite, *Clarissa.*

\* \* \* \*

The sun sets once again
behind the greengrocer's shop.
I move west in my loft
to steal the day's diminished glow
(such is experience).
The lodger's puking child
at last sleeps. The barking spaniel quiets.
Though I feel I must bleed
(there's a goutish pain in my left leg)
my thoughts seem good capital
for setting down.

Most artists, young or old,
when squeezed
yield less blood than a stone.
You were expecting a yawl
anchored in a harbor?
Mine has  H A Y D O N
in gold across its prow
which may not please you
since I have perhaps usurped
your favorite tieing-up slot:
my *placement*, obviously true
to physics and related deportments,
results in your *displacement*.
You must forgive me,
bow to the east, stroke
your cat's throat, then
stroke your self (or your mistress)
and think of me behind the butcher's
chop of time (eighteen 0 nine)
not dissolved entirely by lime.
My words prove it.

I complete Dentatus's head
but am utterly defeated by his sinew.
I attack his back, but fail to hit it!
The Heroic *must* breathe!

Sam is livid and chilled
(I insist on his being nude,
can tell when his mind wanders,
for then his penis hardens, as he
thinks of wenching). I upbraid him,
declaring—and this is true—
a fine model contributes brain-power
to his patron:
I don't strike him,
though my rendering
of the freshly-thrown drapery
is inept.

Fuseli appears (I wish to
choke him!). Deliberately
he seizes chalk
and sketches in a prop,
like one of those that keeps
a house from tumbling.
Laughing, he says,
"Dentatus's leg will break if he falls:
he requires propping.
A maimed hero is no hero at all.
You must *support* him."

I fantasize I grab Fuseli's throat
and choke where high C rolls and trebles.

He departs.
I dash out the prop, all of it,
and know: I must recast the leg
to show the sandal strap
secured to the calf,
I re-pose Sam (he's placated
by a cut of brawn and ham).

Genius is sent into the world
not to obey, but to command!

* * * *

Abstract your sensual appetites.
Assassins
must be *less* assassin-like.
Eschew ugliness.
Academicians will spew disgust.
If you wish to be rich
adore the rich.

* * * *

I'll never wait for anyone,
not even for you.
The swimming baths are closed.

A dream of a surgeon
sawing a man's leg:
the English loathe
Buonaparte's victories.
They invent new densities
of clamoring troops
and erect impossible immensities
of river, scarp, and compagna.
Buonaparte, the genius, sneers.

I sneer at poverty.
I sneer at the middle classes.
I am well-descended, of the gentry.
My uncle sports whiskers.
My aunt wears corset-staves.
I've dined thrice with Mulgrave
who quotes Augustus Pugin:
"Nature must be faithfully rendered."
He sends me armour
from the Tower of London.
Dentatus, indeed, shall be well-garbed.

People of rank and fashion
quit London at Christmas.
I stay behind, alas.
My hunger for an ass-
ignation with a lady of rank
intensifies. My "bone" (ahem)
feels hacked and finished
i.e., useless and unburnished.
No serving wench will do.
Christmas passes (I miss you)
and the New Year brings
fresh cold air and much giggling.
O tender beauties of fashion
and volatile dandies of rank!
Thou shalt thank Dentatus.
Thou shalt thank me!
Fifteen months to paint Dentatus!

Leigh Hunt proceeds with me
(and *Dentatus*) to the Academy.
We shunt the curious aside.
Rounding a corner
I nearly collide
with a lamplighter
about to thrust his ladder
through Dentatus's eye.
I trip the man
and send Dentatus into the gutter.

Fuseli assures me
I'll be well-hung.
Alas, he's over-manned.
I'm relegated to an anteroom.
Lord Mulgrave, as I fear,
falls in with my detractors:
"*Dentatus* would hang better
had it deserved it."

Yet, a few beauties
raise their glasses,
flip their tresses,
and lisp their praises.
A cluster of ambassadors,
speaking French, attend,
I practice an accent,
before approaching them.
Yet, the affair is detestable!
Wilkie (the hit of the exhibition)
shrinks from my defense. What a friend!
He's tapping his foot.
A tram speeds in the wrong direction,
towards Land's End.
I crave to grab off Wilkie
and thrust him up to his neck
in offal!

The devoted artist
deserted as a leper
abused as a felon
and ridiculed by people of fashion
is a madman.
Academies are the curse of art!
Higher life disgusts me.
I'm doomed.

* * * *

Years later I may allow
I've overdone Dentatus—
his expression of contempt—
though his action is good.

Now, Mulgrave must receive the work
since he commissioned it.
In a negative passion
he nails it in a stable
well up under a gable
where it shall lurk for years
bleared by hay-must,
horse-sweat, and grain rust.
I'll scrub it with pumice and a wire brush.

Powder barrels explode
when a woman strikes a pipe
against loose powder.
A cinder-black body
flops over a roof.
Glass shivers into atoms.
Here an arm, there a mutilated trunk.
One man lies halved, another
has his jaw blown off.
I race home bellowing
against Art's coiled vipers,
drink whiskey neat,
and sit until dawn
sketching victims.

# PART TWO

*This Rough World*

My *Macbeth*
perturbs George Beaumont
who faults it.

Lady Macbeth's shadow is complete.
The Lady is not.
Replete are the sleeping grooms,
the sleeping King, and Macbeth
in terror.
Sir George was "in error"
for "requiring" a full-length picture.
I offer a smaller version.
"Not now."
He waves his kerchief with his usual flair,
says he's going for "air."

At home I'm sick:
*Macbeth*'s impasto is too thick.
My model comes. I keep her waiting.
She asks to leave.
"Please yourself."

I thumb *Shakespeare*:
"When in disgrace with fortune and men's eyes."
Aristocratic lies!

I fall asleep on the floor.
Moon-glitter.
The clock strikes four.
I'm walking in my sleep.

An American Negro appears,
a perfect mahogany antique!
I hire him for a month.

What he is is what I see:
a stark body
bent at the loins like whalebone.
His exquisite joints are clean.
I cast him, draw him,
paint every part,
and pull two figures moulded.
He says he's not fatigued
so I mould a third with speed.
His pliant skin allows cracks in.

I mould his back and chest.
We pile on plaster until it sets—seven bushels.
He's afloat up to his neck.

Alas, his ribs have little room
for his lungs to breathe.
"I die—I—I die."

We drive the cast,
draw him forth steaming, struggling
for breath.

We've pulled a perfect form!

A lioness rests
on the heel and ball of her toe
as a human does,
but can't stand erect.
These differences I put
to the animal's brutality,
evidence of man's humanity.

\* \* \* \*

I crave admission to the Royal Academy.
I receive no votes!
Now, in 1810, those livid issues begin
that will torment me until I die.

\* \* \* \*

January 13, 1811. Lost in organ music at the Abbey.

January 14. Paint vigorously. Advance *Macbeth*. I wish the day had 48 hours!

January 16. A fog obscures all light. Have my foot and knee cast for the action of *Macbeth*.

January 19. Nothing. A tormenting dream of Fuseli's *Nightmare*, his boiled-eyed demon poised on my chest.

February 8. Draw at Lord Elgin's for seven hours. Benumbed with cold.

February 15. Draw at Lord Elgin's from six p.m. until eleven.

June 6. Laugh and idle. Walk with Hunt to Primrose Hill. Read Alfieri's memoirs. Idle. Idle.

I attacked the benighted Royal Academy first when I was 26.
Forty Academician hacks were on my back!
(I would be a Martin Luther or John Knox of Art.)
I perplex them:
>I order an even larger canvas and set to work
>on *Solomon and His Judgment.*
>The size will overwhelm them.
I glory in forcing people to do
what I think they ought.
Leigh Hunt jests he'll "slice me into wafers."
I rejoin: I'll crumble him into pounce!
Wilkie, my old friend, does what's expected—
he's in France pursuing "fashion."
My father no longer sends me money, in
or out of season.

* * * *

After months shut up in London
the sea!
Glorious waters beating on a wild shore
with surf!

My sister is with me. We study Italian.
She is unhappy.
Eagles and flags hang from her carriage.
She's swallowed by a turn in the road.

Wind, a dashing rain, and sleet,
a pallet at a wretched inn.
No hot-water bottle for my feet.
Tomorrow, London again!
Six hundred pounds in debt.
I shall sell my books, clothes, everything,
carry my father's watch on a string.
If your wrists are unshackled,
swathe your knees and ankles.
Keep your tibias whittled.
I loiter, entangle with an infernal woman.
Has she the pox?
My brain whirls bats, dead cats,
and salmordines.

\* \* \* \*

Her boy is dashed to pieces
by a horse near Temple Bar.
Her livid lips,
her cheeks are purple,
a glass tear, fixed, without dropping
from her eyelid.
Her screams die
into convulsive sighs.
I paint her as the mother of Solomon.
Measurements are relative:
her grief blots the canvas.

Raphael should *not* have painted small
greasy, leaden easel pictures!
Reject his larger works?
He'd be forgotten.

*Solomon* requires temples, not easels!
Don't tell *me* to paint "small"!

\* \* \* \*

Leigh Hunt and his brother John are imprisoned
for heaping the Prince of Wales with derision.

In their *Examiner*, they avowed the Prince was a liar,
a "fat Adonis of fifty" who can't "tell fat from fire."
I breakfast with them often, to soften their boredom.
Evenings we dine on quail, pears, scones, and mutton.
I depart to clanking chains and crashing pots in the scullery
to spend an evening with Coleridge at the British Gallery.

*Still no dinner.*
Hazlitt our host croaks "Titian."
Hunt is witty.
Lamb stutters quaint incomprehensibilities.
Coleridge emits luxurious poeticalities.
Wilkie chimes in with "Dear, Dear."
*Still no dinner.*
"Hear, hear," we shout.
A maid slaps flatware in a heap.
*Still no dinner.*
Hazlitt orders us to sit, himself
keeps a child at his side.
*Dinner!*
Waxy cold potatoes. A slab of beef
(beyond belief) like a battering-ram, toppling
its corners. Hazlitt's squalling boy, half-clean
screams, stirs gravy with his fingers
and wipes them on Mary Lamb.
In this wainscotted room, alas, Milton meditated,
forced dawn's light through his blinded eyes.
Now, Hazlitt, a mere critic,
admires himself in a glass
and wonders
whether to show more or less
of his forehead.

In England two plus two make four.
In France they would make six
if the national glory required it.
All classes of the French
reflect a martial air.
War is a constituent part
of the national character.
French women have exquisite manners
and hints of beards.
Versailles, pompous and pretentious,
is to be avoided.

A Parisian gentleman
loses a coin in a bearpit.
When an old grenadier creeps in to retrieve it,
the bear eats him.
The French give the bear the veteran's name.
Girls fling sugared buns to the ursine "Martin."
We English would have taken up a subscription.

* * * *

*Solomon* is a critical success,
even among Academicians.
Alas, little did I know
that in thirty years (1844)
*Solomon* would rot in a dust-hole!

Eyes that fail to see
are the eyes of our birth, artery-connected.
The arteries clog.
Why else these flashing lights,
smudged words, lines, and tints?

I am advised to eat nothing but potatoes
avoiding thereby digestive fumes
which, says the apothecary
(I can not afford a doctor),
blear my eyes.

Benjamin West calls, weeps
over the mother in *Solomon*.
He remarks on my sallow skin,
advises more oxygen, purer air,
the avoidance of "external stress."
I seek to hand him his hat
but can not see it.
He bids me farewell.
I panic, send for an apothecary.
He's set to slash my artery,
when Dr. Adams enters,
seizes the knife, flings it from him,
and saves my eyes.
I would be blind surely
had the apothecary
severed the artery.
That night I dine on roast beef, peas,
port wine, sprouts, bread and cheese—
but no, no potatoes!

Wordsworth, you sit to me, thou rugged bard!
These summer weeks I dwell in sight of thee.
I fix the plaster to thy face, and all the while
Thy halcyon thoughts sleep on a tranquil sea.

So pure thy brow, so pure thy hair.
So like, so very like an old Hephaestus every day!
Whene'er I gaze, thy profound Image lurketh there;
When you tire, it trembles, but never sinks away.

Your perfect life-mask seems to sleep.
A mood, which winter takes away, or brings:
I fancied (and still do) the mighty Deep
gentles when you sleep.

Ah! do forgive the rudeness of my Painter's hand
To capture bliss and add the elusive gleam:
The genius of your face that never was ere this, on sea or land,
The abomination of all pain, the Poet's dream.

I will not torture thee, thou hoary Pile.
(Forgive the parallel.)
Near thy immortal face that always smiles
Recumbent lie my brushes, easel, and my file.

Thou art to us a treasure house divine
Of wisdom, a testament of Heaven—
Of all the sun (and moon)beams that do shine
The choicest have to thee (and us) been given.

The portrait I do paint of thee, dear Soul,
emits an Elysian quiet, without strife.
It is so true, as all the world opines,
thy spirit profound is Nature's silent life.

Receive this passionate, imperfect work.
I am a hulk who labors in the deadly swell of earth,
in confrontation with fierce winds and trampling waves:
thy portrait, Poet, is a Birth!

The greatest *coup de main*—
Napoleon's return from Elba.
He violated constitutional law,
was inordinately anxious
to possess the King of Rome,
was too enamored of his dynasty,
which the French (*les gens*)
were not anxious to preserve.
When he abdicated we felt contempt.
When he rushed to Paris
we shrank in the presence of a comet.
His destruction prostrates Hazlitt,
who walks about unwashed, unshaven,
much intoxicated for weeks.
Then Hazlitt restores himself, assumes
his earlier populist principles.
The Duke of Wellington
is our Wordsworth of battle.
He saved the intellect of the world,
the soldier as poet swaying the universe.

\* \* \* \*


Alas, at my age Raphael had completed a room
in the Vatican! I content myself moulding
the feet of horsemen on the Elgin marbles,
and am frightened over my poor eyes, my diet,
and over cash for canvas, models, and paints.

*January*, 1816:
After four months of misery
I return to painting.
The colors rise with buttery firmness.
My fingers revel.
I seize my maul-stick,
insert thumb through palette,
and mounting my table,
dash in a head, sing, shout, and whistle,
thanking God.

These, Dr. Darling says, caused my blindness:
indigestion, a deranged liver,
hard thinking, bad feeding,
the foul air in my painting-room.

         * * * *

Payne Knight, that arbiter of taste,
collector of bronzes and intaglios,
begins a horrid imbroglio
and debases the Elgin marbles.

Whilst Elgin is a prisoner in France
Knight delivers his wretched opinion—
the sculptures are mediocre Endymions
of inferior stone, not worth a pittance:

"They're not Greek, they're Roman,
of the time of Hadrian. Or else, if Attic,
they're by Callicrates.

"Elgin should not have raised them
when their ship struck a boulder
and they sank through the water.
The event was truly a Divine stratagem.

"Lord Byron avers that transporting these works
was a vandalizing desecration,
and not, per Elgin the *paronomasia*,
a 'rescue' from the destructive Turks.

"The Parthenon now, that violated fane,
the pride of Pericles and Cecrops,
enhances the Beauty of London chimney-pots:
we certainly know where to lock the chain.

"Members of Parliament, do not be dissuaded.
The Nation's in dire financial need.
Do not be toothless, withhold your meed:
this project is much too well-oiled and pomaded.

"Ignore Elgin's lackey Benjamin Haydon.
His nine-page letter, almost hysterical,
rises to heights obscene and fantastical,
Haydon's no cannon; he's a miserable popgun."

In 1816, on the seventh of June,
by a vote of eighty-two to thirty
Parliament performed its awesome duty
outvoting the insensitive clods and poltroons.

The Nation paid Elgin some forty thousand,
against his costs of seventy thousand.
Haydon's new enemies were rich and numerous.
They decreed him scurrilous, bibulous,
curious, and ludicrous.

A burglar has stolen my ears:
I'm in love!

In a small drawing room
sits a young wife in a cherry rocking chair.
On a sofa a man is dying. . . .
I can't write, eat, or sleep.
Books, pictures, and marbles bore me.
O, Mary Hyman!

At her husband's funeral,
I touch her warm white hand in passing
(will I ever wash it again, my hand?)
Can I live without her?

She *will* be my wife!
I'm so in love.
Will she give me her husband's breeches?
Wrap the dead man's cravats
in the *Illustrated News*?
My *Lazarus* is cold mutton.

John Keats visits my painting-room.
He's of middle-size,
with a low forehead, eyes
with the inward look
of a Delphian priestess given to visions.
"Fix your eye on the horizon, Haydon."
He hopes to discover
"the human dusthole"
where his dead brother lies.

Keat's voice is feminine.
Shelley's is masculine.
Keats falls ill and shortly dies.
I saw him for the last time in his bed,
hectic and on his back.
He had few hopes, stretched on life's horrid wrack.
To intensify his appetite,
he whitened his tongue and throat with pepper,
the better to savor cold claret.
He appears in my *Christ Entering Jersualem*
with Wordsworth, Lamb, and Hazlitt.

Three Life Guardsmen transport my painting.
The frame weighs six hundred pounds.
An iron ring snaps.
We raise it into place by machinery.
Now, for the glazing. . . .
Sir George Beaumont, bless him,
gives thirty pounds, which sees me through.

Sarah Siddons sails in,
a fantastic Ceres or Juno
overwhelming and awing all present.
When asked delicately
if she likes my Christ,
she replies in her deepest, loudest,
most tragical tone: "It is successful."
She invites me to her home,
her voice is awful and intimidating.

She reads Macbeth, taking all the parts.
We have tea, toast, and tarts.
She begins again.
We slink into our seats like boors,
with toast in our mouths, afraid to bite,
afraid of crackling.

A servant observes proudly:
"She tunes her pipes as well as she ever did."
A clangorous mass bell in Madrid.

I'm wrong to paint so huge!
I'm wrong to choose a theme
to be hung where quadrilles are danced!
Yet, I always fill my painting-room.
If I owned a room 400' long, 200' high,
and 400' wide that would decide
the size of *Lazarus*.

\* \* \* \*

Of a conversazione of celebrated men
Samuel Johnson said: "not one but would feel pain
at his own reflections before midnight."
Tested daily
we are seldom found sound.
I worry about the Sacred Book of Art
as a dog worries a ram's bone.
Imagine plunging into a tomb
in a desert say . . . in the Sahara.
When you find a scarab
take a pinch of snuff, coolly,
as a touch of nature!

A tomb is a good place for a harem
because women should have something important
to look at.

* * * *

Something rustles. A being buried in satin and diamonds
    rolls gravely forth.
The coronation room rises with a feathered, silken thunder.
Plumes wave, eyes sparkle, glasses are out, mouths smile,
    and one man
George IV becomes the object of attraction to thousands.
Flower girls precede him, milky, shining in sunlight.
Distant trumpets, shouts, the King crowned beneath a
    canopy of gold.
A man would go mad if mortality did not occasionally hold
    up a mirror. The Queen is the death's head at this feast.

I am linked wrist to wrist
ankle to ankle in marriage
             to an angel.

Mary Hyman and I exchange vows
on October 10, 1821. I start with
             two step-children.

Women are angels sent from heaven
to temper the fire and furious energy
             of men into gentler paths.

The finest sight on earth is to see Mary
as consciousness wafts over her face
             in the morning.

I am fortune's sport—up in one freak
and bowled down in another. I astonish
             the world by leaping forth again.

Her smile is an angel's in a sunny dream.
She's nearby as I pen this
             and is laughing.

Three arrests for debt in a single day.
Bewick is sitting as Lazarus.
             Knocks at the door.

I dismiss the boor and return to Bewick.
Lazarus's head! Egad, Bewick! I have it!
The best head I've ever painted!

I berate my creditor, a miserable apothecary.
My wife may miscarry.
Where is my attorney?
Mary presses her face to my lips
as if she grows to my form.

* * * *

A throttled scream,
an infant's cry,
Mrs. Thatham standing by.
"It's a boy!"
My beloved Frank is born!
(Dec. 12th, 1822)

* * * *

March 1, 1823: the private day. No picture I have painted is
so enthusiastically received as *Lazarus.*
March 3: despite wind and rain, the picture succeeds.
March 4: receipts double today.
March 5: the impression continues.
March 6: the receipts increase!
March 7: I begin to sketch my massive *Crucifixion*, settling
the perspective and the primary compositional lines.
April 1: the receipts still up. Creditors howling and baying.
April 13: an execution put in on *Lazarus.*
April 18: officials conduct a hurried inventory of my
possessions.
April 21: I am arrested.
April 22: I am in prison. My wife joins me there.
April 28: a meeting of my creditors, followed by a petition
to the House of Commons for my release.
July 23: I face the Insolvent Court. Not one of my 150
creditors opposes me. I am acquitted.
July 25: I am free!

# PART THREE

*Bread and Ashes*

Mary is birthing again.
I desire the vegetable husk of a prostitute.
There's a dribble of blood on my finger.

I hate vampires.
Death thoughts are sexual.
The blotched carrot-scrapings of my life,
mucus-cold leeks.
And these dead friends:
Scott to a duel, Fuseli, Keats. . . .
I once knew much
of life's allegorical buskins,
satins, voiles, and silk-skins
in a withering landscape
(oh, is that a beech?) of frozen glass.

*  *  *  *

Yes, a crenellated castle
where I'll live when I'm rich.
My fingers bleed as I lick them.
Poverty swells our bellies
in this greasy time.
Mary's had neither chine
nor fowl this week.
Frank has lost his hair.
News of life, news of death.

*Silenus*, my last hope, does not sell.
Four children and a wife require food.
Portraits over the Heroic Style?
The mayor of Plymouth as an ancient Senator?
I shall be ridiculed.
I work willy-nilly.

*Portrait!*
The more intelligible an action
the less reason for a vigorous facial expression.
"Some men there are love not a gaping pig.
Some go mad if they behold a cat."
Oh, these trifles!
I resent my family.
I'm a miserable father.
I ache for bachelorhood.
To feel common is to be common!

My demons' fingers are black and bony.
I stand before a dead grate (no money)
with brush in hand, incapable
of slapping the impasto
where it ought to go.

Our bullying, insolent landlady,
an evil-eyed, wrinkled, waddling,
gin-soused, dirty-ruffled bit
of asthmatic humanity. . . .

When a rascal serves debtor papers
turn him to the light.
The effect is never questionable.

A prison turnkey in the glare.
His mean face is blotched with drink and soil.
A feeble nose, brassy eyes, a neck boil,
low forehead, and a fetid smell:
a reptile.

A dream:
I flee a crowd who also flee.
"Haydon escapes from prison!
He's beserk, armed with knives and razors!"

Through letters and sheer persistence
I hope to persuade Parliament
to engage painters to adorn public buildings.
"Geniuses are lettuces," I say.
"Nurture them!"

Turner's painting of Trafalgar
disgusts the Commission so
they vow to hire no more painters.

As I paint a head
and revel in color
and hit an expression
I sit down fatigued
and read a poet and am relieved.
I wake as from a foggy dream
to persistent grime and steam
(Ah, this shrill world!).
I ache for a competence,
a mountain stream, a rill,
a library, a painting-room,
and the means to educate my children.

Thomas Stothard, R. A.
is in gaol as bail for another.
"What a game we throw, dear friend," I say.
"Our cards are fruitless,
as were Homer's, Tasso's, and Galileo's.
We lack pitch else we'd be rich
like Landseer or Eastlake (my pupils),
or Lawrence, or West."

*Moses leading 600,000 Israelites.*
I search the British Museum
for everything Egyptian:
architectural orders,
miniature humans in funeral boats,
acanthuses, brief costumes.
I must not cheat.
The work must be discreet.
I paint a moon and sky.
The moon reflects a varied light
else it's a shilling.
The backs of my eyes pain—
a sign I dread.
I go to bed, in fits:
fits of work,
fits of idleness,
fits of reading,
fits of walking,
fits of Napoleon,
fits of Greek,
fits of Latin,
fits of Egyptian,
fits of the army,
fits of the navy,
fits of religion.
Dear Mary's face
is the only fit
that never varies.

December 5, 1825, 3 a.m.
Alfred Haydon born.
I *shall* rear my boys as gentlemen!

I waft a sweet-scented breeze
towards the Academy
which has improved, it seems to me.

I slide in on bended knee
hoping that the aristocracy
will at long last welcome me.

I eschew my wonted hostility
and gratify the malignant discontentedly.
I crave harmony.
They clap their hands, go free.

I send them *Venus and Anchises.*
Again, I'm rejected:

> *Old Alcibiades*
> *lopped off a dog's tail*
> *to make people wail.*

* * * *

At the Riding School, a Life Guardsman
strips and rides fiercely.
I halt him where the King would stand.
Hind and fore quarters, and the neck pulled in.
Alexander *must* look a youth
else the gist be lost.
He's a long-forked Life Guardsman.
He's not quite good enough!

Chalk-in Alexander's head
then rub it out.
I seldom alter work but to repent.

Observe the green cresting the meadow.
Tall lilacs and lilies blow.
Peaceful and holy, no duns, no letters,
no snooty missives from my Academy "betters."

Shall I pawn Homer, Vasari,
Shakespeare, or Tasso?
No!
Simply to *see*
the backs of books by men of genius. . .
I am fonder of books
than anything else on earth!

* * * *

Soirees and matinees!
Women screw their mouths in pouts
Men suck their lips to redden them.
The trash we talk!
My mind rots
craving an entry.
I loathe soirees and matinees.

January and February - Law and harassed.
March - Hard work and harassed.
April - Sketched and harassed.
May - Ill and harassed.
June - Begin *Alexander* again.
July - Hard at work and harassed.
August - Hard at work.
September - Hard at work and harassed.
October - Ill and harassed.
November - To Brighton, and harassed.
December - Finish *Alexander*. More harassed by the law than
 ever.

The childen cry louder
the postman knocks harder
the dustman's bell is noisier
I crouch gaping at the weather.

* * * *

My poorest student (and the best) is Lough, a sculptor.
He's so ill-fed he's giddy.
A bushel of coal must last the winter.
He sleeps on the floor curled
against his clay model, although the model is damp.

He completes *Ceres*, exhibits it.
Mrs. Siddons is ecstatic.
I'm so delighted with his success
I can't proceed with my own painting!

In 1827, I hope to see:
  1. My debts paid.
  2. Historical painting endowed by the Government.
  3. The American navy thrashed.

* * * *

June, 1827, again, imprisoned.
Four thousand pounds!
Mary pawns our silver and her wedding clothes.
I part with all books but Shakespeare.
*A sixth child.*
Lord Gower convenes a public meeting
at the Crown and Anchor Tavern.
Three hundred pounds are subscribed.

Hopes are boundless,
miseries are endless.
The world is a prison
of large dimensions.
My torso is stripped.
Summers are infinite.
Does it matter I'm rejected?
Adore the eagle in his flight.
At no table rich or poor
does one man bless another.
Sail to new worlds,
then (ridiculous) return to the point
you've departed from.
I consider my body
and wish to burn it.
I scribble in my journal
disguised as another person,
a shiek of Araby! Satan's Infernal!
Today has more zeroes than usual.

* * * *

A man like myself,
though the town rings
with his afflictions,
thinks mainly of painting.

A man who has never observed a face
without wishing to limn it,
would probably, even at the stake,
study the miens of his executioners.

Holt the pugilist sits.
His hair springs like wire.
Next, a coy puppy should win all hearts.
The public will love *The Mock Election*.

September 10: Advanced my puppy.
September 11: Advanced and improved my puppy.
September 12: Finished the velvet cap of the puppy. I take
    much delight in this puppy.

* * * *

King George V says he'll buy *Mock Election*.
I am so inured to being in prison one day,
and in a palace the next,
I am not moved.

* * * *

How can I believe anything?
Bumping into chairs,
overturning candles.
My dear Frank's lungs are inflamed.
I grip his bed as he doubles in pain.
He sweats.
He gazes up, a fellow-string
of the same instrument.
I am startled, dozing.
I'll paint a *Punch*.
Frank's feeble voice recalls me.
I have no orders, no commissions.

# PART FOUR

*This World's Cruel Wrack*

Swells and diapasons
and a stream
in the country of indifference.
There's room for my big toe only
which I insert.
One's sucking my breast.
It's my mother, or Frank,
or my new daughter.

My path is perilous.
I pass the point of reversing myself.
Lady Lyndhurst's hands
as Sir Thomas Lawrence paints them
are a disgrace.
Yet he's rich!

A hazlenut copse.
The sky is a nun's wimple pastel-hued.
That denuded hill requires a bandage.
Kick the sheep aside and proceed.
Don't summon a cabriolet
or the hackman whipping his team:
the pain of
nothing in your tree,
or a scream on top of a wedding cake.

The Duke of Wellington
declines "permission"
for any work "whatsoever"
dedicated to him.

Don't writhe with laughter at my woes.
Like yours, they began somewhere ('tis true?).
Don't pick your nose! Don't scratch your eye!
The depths are smart, the heights mis-
chosen. Plinths and pediments flake and peel.
Little people squeal and deal.
That's the fashion.
The moon is rancid.

You think you are winning
at least you proceed
towards Lord So-and-So's fête-tent.
The warm lemonade
the cucumber charade
cretonnes in the shade
the tunes replayed
on tinkling spinets. Deranged
Sir and Lady Disastrous
wrinkled by winds
near the lily pond.
Her Ladyship modulates
miasmic trebles, chic,
pastel exquisites, iced vocables
sweetened tea.
Why do we care?
Roses near a stone bench.
Don't whack them down!
The bailiff orders peace,
his truncheon bangs cacophonies
on iron chains and keys.

* * * *

A shepherd's dog
is the model for my *Punch*.
Such simple things amaze,
that a dog's life is eternal.
My heart's slow drip.
The diurnal drizzle.
A widow's (my dear Mary's) weeds.

Sir Thomas Lawrence is dead.
That toady of taste and fashion.

He drew with incorrectness
to suit the season.

His women were rich or wanton.
His gentlemen were dandies.
His children insipid.

His necks were hideously long,
waists tiny, chests puffed
and ankles tapered beyond reason.

His early works, God knows,
were the scrapings of a tin-smith,
sparkles without repose.

He always submitted.
His smile was enamel.
It could have been silver.

Nature's sweet bloom and cunning
never laid hold on him.
He died before he began.
I'll not attend his funeral.

Imprisoned again!
A prison is a perfect world
compressed in a narrow space.

I love England's beef, its boxing,
and its "bottom."
I'll never leave, as my friends advise.

Incarcerations are always tentative,
so I make the most of them.

The King's gunmaker is imprisoned too:
he has the slang of fashion, without the excuse.

Divinity and "harbal" cures
are the head turnkey's passion.

He gathers curative plants
"under the planets"
and feeds prisoners from his own table.

A nobleman and a boy-stunner
are reclining on straw pallets.
The latter sips brandy
and seems of good cheer.

My own son Orlando is at Oxford.
(To keep him there I'm twice imprisoned.)
Dear Frank, my eldest, visits me distressed.
Mary is dejected.
We exchange minimal variations of feeling.

I am released.
I paint for the first time in eleven weeks.
I relish the oil
and taste the alizarin,
rub my cheeks with the brushes
and kiss the palette.
I crave to adorn the new House of Lords!
Alas, my enemies!

* * * *

The King turned livid
and dropped his head and said
"This is death," and died.

N.B. Another son is born:
*Benjamin Robert Haydon.*

Ideas flow by the million!
O, the muck in the art-shop windows.

Mary comforts our sick children—
Three may be dying—
and hushes the pair still suckling.

Out selling prints all day.
The dealer rests his hand in mine,
as does the beggar.

I buy shoes for Mary, and a dinner!
The world jiggles on
as we grow thinner.
How many are we?
Thirteen?
That's ten more than I can feed, I ween.

A heavenly choir
kisses my slumber
as a new day slips forth.
A moth on my mouth feeds on spittle.
It traverses my lip,
my cheek, and my startled eye.
It sips water from my lid
then treks over my forehead.
I pluck it
without damaging the delicate wings.

My brain swelters.
I swoon and slumber.
A voice of dinner pans.
Spine-chilling rattlings
of femurs and tibias
drifting, it seems,
over the Atlantic.
A tinted lea
a cloisonné stream.
I stand at my easel
beneath a willow tree.
Clappers tinkling inside lilies.
Two, no three, children,
their feet tangled in bluebells. . . .
"Papa! Papa!"
They're my dead children!
Their finger-bones interlace, their
skulls have shreds of hair, their
jaws are agape.
Hummingbirds of blood
well from their throats!
I'll not be tricked again!
I'll hasten! I'll hasten to join them!

*Jerusalem* goes to America.
My son at Oxford lives on bread and water.
Wordsworth writes a sonnet for my *Napoleon on St. Helena.*

\* \* \* \*

On board a Greek ship
sailing at a merry clip
Byron stroked a Turk's yatagan
and rocked and swayed
until the warrior, dismayed,
sheathed up the sword again.
Now Byron is dead, felled by a fever
as I, wretch, break bread and eat my dinner.
Said Byron: "I declare, I wish to share
a murderer's feelings laid bare."
Inflamed by lutes and mandolins
excesses wore him thin.
I love his verse, I envy his name,
I wish he'd been moral, and not lame.

My children are fighting.
Mary is weeping.
No water in the cistern.
No milk in the scullery.
No twigs on the fire.

The room's a cavern.
There's a southern breeze,
so we won't freeze.
I'm forty-seven today,
a fact no one mentions.

This evening passes as always
where the father has no money.
Cups of kindness,
tea, and irritability.
The lynx-eyes of my children.
"The man says he wishes he could,
but he won't leave any firewood
until he has his money."

Death comes
pounding a drum.
Each night curled in bed
I pray I'll wake dead.

My Harry, there he lies
a lad of gifts and enterprise.
He'd pore for hours over
prints of *Napoleon Musing*.
Now, here comes the mortician.

I sketch Harry in his coffin.
His gorgeous head!
"His day without a cloud was passed,
And he was lovely to the last."

Mary begs from a friend
to pay for his funeral.
I take my best engravings,
rub out the names
and garner five pounds more.
We earn three pounds on
pots, pans, and clothing—
goods we'll never see again.

Rubbed in John Milton at his organ.
Milton and his daughter hawking *Paradise Lost*.
Eloise and Abelard reciting St. Thomas Aquinas.
Dear Mary at her looking-glass.
Orestes hesitating to murder Clytemnestra.
Lord Grey musing.
Rubbed in Mr. Cowper and Mrs. Leicester Stanhope.
Read Mignet's *History of the French Revolution*.
My estimate of Napoleon: A dead hero
grows in the hearts of his adorers.

Oh, to end it all, by my own hand
(I whisper this to you).
Little Georgy dies in much pain
from a brain suffusion.
I try to sketch her, but refrain.

Funeral lilacs and forsythia
rusticated brick
my baby son's sweet neck—
no re-beginnings.
We are what we become.
I'll hurl this wretched business down
and jump from a parapet!

"Haydon, Sir: you have thought proper to procure from my servant one of my very own coats, with trousers, without any order or consent on my part, for your *picture*. Now you expect me to inspect same, to give approval, so that you may sell more when it is engraved. Further, to paint the Emperor Napoleon on the rock of St. Helena is quite a different thing from painting me on the field of the Battle of Waterloo. The Emperor did not consent to be painted. I am, however, supposed to consent. I have the honour to be, Sir, Your most obedient, humble servant, WELLINGTON. February 7, 1835."

* * * *

In a dream
I sail with Wellington
through the Latitudes.
I strip, plunge in and swim,
as a wild youth.
I skim through froth
towards an enormous curling wave.
Mary is there. Will she be saved?
Was she here before?
I return to shore.

An horrendous lightning.
The wave breaks, to the left,
on the shingles.

Marcus Curtius darts into my head.
I shall paint Curtius
leaping into the abyss.

On May 16, 1836
Newton my youngest dies.
My commitments to lecture
at Oxford (where I am honored),
Liverpool, Edinburgh, Manchester,
and London (at the Mechanics
and Royal Institution) revive me.

I never fear an audience,
illustrate my remarks
with drawings, rapidly
and vigorously thrown,
am humorous, excited, benign,
by turn and turn about.
I use two nude wrestlers
to show muscle groups in motion,
which occasions sniggers and laughter.
"Respect the Almighty's handiwork,"
I thunder. Silence thereafter.
I fashion the homely equation:
the ellipsis shaping a milk-jug
shaped the heroic limbs of the Ancients.

In Edinburgh I gain the upper classes
and am spared the profferings
of insipid amateur drawings,
normal after my lectures.
My lecture on the nude
(I pay my wrestlers to struggle)
draws 1500 people. Two decades ago
this was impossible.
The lectures receive my full attention.
May the Queen grant me a pension.
I'm nearly fifty-two.
What else must my family go through?
I am unable to temper
vengeful allusions to the Academy.

When a man touches my property
I pay the claim.
When he seizes my person
I let the law take its course, as I ever shall.

* * * *

My Mary's son Simon dies upon the brine
    Bitten by a seven-foot reptile
On the Indian Ocean, while aboard the brig *Algerine*.

A sailor thinks he's hooked a crocodile.
    Simon grabs the serpent's folds
An action rash and juvenile.

The asp is the color of marigolds
    With forty black rings evenly spaced.
It pierces his metacarpal bones, and holds.

Thank God, it's not his face.
    The first of his pains are minimal.
At breakfast during grace

His throat feels like rock-crystal.
    Giddiness, dizziness, and a few temblors.
He's dead after a short interval.

A medical man remembers
    That Simon's spotted body
Slipped into the sea at vespers.

The snake all skinned and potted
    Had two small rows of teeth
orange, broken, worn, and rotted.

Gentle Simon now rests above.
    We send his brother his clothes
and you our love.

The Queen! The Queen!
on the road to Hounslow,
whither I am wending.
I jerk off my spectacles,
press my hat upon my head,
and wait for vantage.

First come the Lancers
then her outriders.
Prince George *sees*,
but does not *know* me.

                    \* \* \* \*

I *have* the Duke of Wellington!
I don't require his clothes.
A tailor makes facsimiles.
   Duke, I've beat *you*.
   I *do* you
   despite you!
   For the background
   I'll visit Waterloo.
   Your gloved hand requires
   a hint of milky blue.
*He* hopes there'll be
"A cessation of notes about pictures to me."

My Anti-slavery Convention canvas:
Fourteen sketches in a day.

Lucretia Mott leads the American women,
has infidel notions, so I do not give her
the prominence I intended:
that goes to a devout Believer.

I try to ascertain Lloyd Garrison's heart,
hit him, and he meets me directly.
A man, he says, who places the Negro level
must relish sitting by his side.

Sketched Lady Byron, capturing
her sorrow, lambent and touching.
She was no more fit for Lord Byron
than a skylark for a volcano.

Worked at Charles Birney:
"Negro children equal whites
until they are seven. Then, alas,
their parents' degradation degrades them."

No one buys the picture.
I am disastrous, in arrears.

I see *Solomon* again,
after twenty-seven years.
Damp has eaten Solomon's robe
as well as his crown.
The crown was painted
in India yellow, a vegetable.
Since I painted the drapery in lake,
(an animal substance),
mildew flakes it.
The remainder, in earths
or minerals, is unaffected.
Solomon's face is pure
amidst the mildew.

I'm fit for better worlds!
Since *this* world won't honor me
I'll go to a new one shortly.

To relieve our diseased brains
we trick ourselves
into self-destruction
and betray what must not be betrayed,
a vegetable life splattered
over a Turkey carpet.

A fevered brain requires a horrid crime.
A slimy ruse, worse
than fish sauce, worse
than pustulent exudations. . . .

My memories clang
like silver bells.
No vicar
nor dram of liquor
can ever put this right.
I shall not die tonight.

The Houses of Parliament competition:
cartoons on the history of Britain.
I'm confident of winning,
so am learning *fresco*.
I'm sixteen again!

Eastlake cautions: Don't fantasize.
The prize may not materialize.
His Committee will name the winners.
I covet this commission.

Lime and marble-dust
sand and slime, in equal parts.
Slap the concoction on the wall
to see what cracks, what adheres,
and what falls.

I loathe *fresco*:
To have a color dry one thing
when you've meant it for another!
The flesh seams in the shadows!
To copy a cartoon
once your fire has dimmed . . . Oho,
would frustrate Michelangelo!

It's night.
There's a horrid sameness
to my inventions.
I fume facing *Saragossa.*

"Eat," says Hunger,
misgauging my desire
for meat and gin.
What a world!
A touch of madder here,
ultramarine there,
defining musket and bayonet.
Are my eyes that poor?
It's all the same color!
I kick the bayonet.
While waiting for the surgeon,
I paint the foreground.
Never lose an opportunity.

Wordsworth dozes in church
beside a servant in livery.
I jog him awake at the Gospel.

He's eight heads high (to my wonder),
i.e., 5 ft. 9 7/8 in., and of
heroic proportions.
He has me write the measurements
for Mrs. Wordsworth.

His inflamed eye
requires
that he sit in one light,
a light I despise
since it smarts my eyes.
Yet, the sketch succeeds.
He comes again tomorrow
with or without false teeth,
the former, I hope.

My mind is not obscene:
I love nobility,
and I love horses.
I love velleities, and, most of all
I love my daughter Mary.
Yes, horses
both colossal and miniature,
subjected to the rowels of men,
run rampant over stiles, or through the skies.
In battle, fear scums their flanks like mucus.
Striken, shafted through the withers
their stunned eyes mist and quiver.
They crumble.
That's how it happens, spinning round a pin,
avoiding the rush of adrenalin. . .
We are both brute (brutal) and bruitish!
There's always more speed in the light
than in shadows. Let me finish . . .
   *That's not the brass knocker.*
   *Don't expect me to open the door!*
My love for athletes and muscular dragoons
relates to equine forms.
Poise a man (a Napoleon say)
astride a horse.
Both are aggrandized
by cannon and musket smoke.
The gluteus maximus—
that incredible muscle
of endurance, sex,
and the prowess of both
human and Pegasusian bodies.
The man becomes the horse,
larger than life,
hence, nobler.

I don't appear among the muralists
for the Houses of Parliament.
Carriages squeeze past my window
up to their hubs in treacle.
"Beware the happy man."
Curtius is my mirror!
His rage is mine!
I am Curtius
on his white steed.
Noble Curtius,
caparisoned in splendor,
gesticulates to Heaven,
leaps on his stallion

I paint *my* life!
They'll never tame this white stallion!

\* \* \* \*

So, you'd like a libation?
I'm sorry I can't offer you ale.
It's a question of milk
for a sick wife and children.

The citizens of London are windows painted black.
There's still some evening.
I'll pawn our silver butter-knife,
then visit Elizabeth Barrett.
We'll share some claret.
She'll keep my papers safe.
I'll burn all other letters,
to keep them from my "betters."
They'll never *sell* my pictures
to pay my debts!
*Curtius! Curtius! Curtius!*

\* \* \* \*

A tamed lion with hideous fangs
leans his head aside whilst I pat him.
I soothe his paw and stroke his hirsute jaw.
His lioness, in heat, pats my pate.
Luckily, I wear a hat, or
I might be knocked senseless.
I sketch these creatures for a new painting.

I love my silent, midnight ways.
Yet, the majesty of High Art eludes me.
The paltry flicker of farthing candles
dims a steady fire.
I am beset.
Another arrest.
Hayricks where my dear dead children play.
Young people marry who were then scarce born.
My terrible needs lie unresolved.

I'll paint Satan!
I'll reflect so much Evil my viewers shall tremble!

I proceed, ecstatic, smearing half-tints,
amazing lights, amazing darks.

Alas, I've no more madder
(for Satan's complexion).
A wretched pass!

\* \* \* \*

Colonel Gurwood has slashed his throat!
That rigid soldier,
the iron-nerved hero!
Our minds, 'tis clear, usurp our bodies.
My headaches tell me this,
I refuse, adamantly refuse, to listen!

I have lost nearly seven hundred pounds
on my last six exhibitions.
I shall rent a hall,
keep the admission minimal.
Barnum exhibits General Thumb.
Hordes trampling to see Thumb
must pass my gallery, and some,
I am confident, will, *must* enter.
I dare them to avoid me! Come
what may, this is my last hope.

"*Burning of Rome by Nero.*
*The Banishment of Aristides.*
Haydon's drawing is grand,
the characters most felicitous"—THE TIMES. .
"Haydon's best work. He has
devoted forty-two years to improving
British taste."—THE HERALD.
"*Let every Briton with pluck in his bosom*
*and a shilling in his pocket*
*crowd to these works during Easter week.*"

The private day: incessant rain.
   They push
   They fight
   They scream
   They faint
   They cry help and murder!
And oh and ah
      *Over Tom Thumb.*
My bills
My boards
My caravans
My pictures
      *They ignore.*
An insanity
A madness
A rabies
A furor
      *Their eyes are open, their senses barred.*

95

Tom Thumb's first week
gains six thousand pounds.
B.R. Haydon's week: five pounds,
thirteen shillings, and sixpence,
based on visits of 133½ persons,
the half being a little girl.
An unkind cut:
Dickens tramps the stairs to Thumb,
but never crosses over to my exhibition!

No funds to pay for the Hall.
A broker threatens imprisonment.
The landlord demands a quarter's rent.
The cook upbraids me for her pay.
My heart sinks, my brain flails—
a sting-ray in death-throes.

I apply strokes to my new *Alfred*.
I fire up, then throw the palette
in disgust. I sleep on the floor
and wake irritable.

Mary writes to son Frederic
sailing on *The Grecian* to South America.
She writes verses:
    "This is thy natal day, my child:
        And where are thou so dear?
    My heart is sad, and yet 'tis glad
        To know thou art not here."

May 18: I lose £111
   on my exhibition. I depart Egyptian Hall,
   a skillful retreat,
   before General Thumb. I'm a beaten exhibitor.

* * * *

   My soul aspires
   My spirit is wounded
   My hand fumbles
   My heart races
   My brain aches to burst
   My hand drops the impasto-laden brush
   My eyes wail hot tears
   I fail to shave, to wash
   to change my linen
The glory of being a painter
resides in one's utter neglect
by critics and public.

* * * *

I ask friend L----
for £100. We dine in the city
on mutton, wine, and trifle.
Laughter is a patina.
O God, Thy will be done!
He breaks the news: bad times
prevent his advancing even a threepence.

At home I drink much, the only time,
my Mary says, she's seen me so.
The hottest, most airless summer
on record, "a sultry month."
I do not sleep, except in fits.
I stare like an idiot at *Alfred.*
The paint on his face is cold gravy.
I write to Lord Peel, Beaufort, and Brougham.
Nothing avails.

I burn more letters and papers, pack up
my valuables, what might be sold as income—
the drawings of Wellington, Wordsworth,
my wife and dead children,
plus a metal box containing journals—
and carry all to Elizabeth Barrett.
She'll keep them from my creditors—
she's promised.

Miss Barrett, in purple,
reclines on a sofa.
(The evening is stifling.)
Flush sleeps in her lap.
She strokes him as she is speaking.
I'm lost in a wish to sketch her,
am abstracted rehearsing the line
round her thin mouth, the cheek bones,
the tendrils of hair scooping her temples. . . .

"If only I could die," I exclaim,
"there'd be a subscription
(I trust the English people)
to support my family."

Monday, June 22, 1846.
Stop at Riviere, the gun-maker, in Oxford Street.
Purchase one of a pair of small pistols.
At 9, I breakfast alone, then go to my painting-room.
I write letters to my children,
re-write my will, and sketch some final thoughts.
As usual, I lock myself in.
My daughter Mary, my confidante
(more even than her mother)
suspects nothing when she tries the door.
She says (through the door) that
she and her mother are going out.
"Very well," I say.
Impulsively, I go to her,
kiss her fervently, and linger.
There is something I wish to say.
But I walk away.

I load the pistol, poise a lone straight-razor near.
It's 10:45. I face the door.
Noise in the street. The hot air is a pall.
I squeeze the trigger.
Its small caliber deflects along the bone.
Why, even now, must I fail! Desperate
(for Mary will hear)
I grab up the open razor
and slice my throat, from ear to ear.
  *Finis. Benjamin Robert Haydon.*

# NOTE

Mary Haydon accompanies her mother part of the way to Brixton, returns, and hastens to her father's painting-room to console him. In the subdued light nothing is clear. She is struck by the loud ticking of her father's watch on a table. She looks for her father, but he is not there.

His *Journals* lie open on the table, and there are sealed letters, and a prayer book she had given him. A recently completed portrait of herself stands on an easel.

She walks further into the room and finds him lying on the floor. She believes he is down so as to study some aspect of his *Alfred*. When she calls he does not answer. She calls softly again, and sees that he is huddled on the floor. Her floot slips in what she thinks is red paint—it is his blood. For a moment, Mary's heart stops beating.

Her father lies with his head half resting on his right arm. His face is greenish white. Across his neck are two frightful gashes, in different directions. She is standing in her father's blood.

Mary never recovers from the shock, and dies in 1864, ten years after her mother.